# my home in the desert

By J. Patrick Lewis

Children's Press®
An Imprint of Scholastic Inc.

Library of Congress Cataloging-in-Publication Data

Names: Lewis, J. Patrick.
Title: My home in the desert/by J. Patrick Lewis.
Description: New York, NY : Children's Press, [2017] | Series: Rookie poetry.
Animal homes | Includes index.
Identifiers: LCCN 2016030841| ISBN 9780531228715 (library binding) | ISBN
9780531230060 (pbk.)
Subjects: LCSH: Desert animals—Juvenile literature.
Classification: LCC QL116 .L49 2017 | DDC 591.754—dc23
LC record available at https://lccn.loc.gov/2016030841



Produced by Spooky Cheetah Press
Design by Anna Tunick


Printed in China 62



1 2 3 4 5 6 7 8 9 10 R 26 25 24 23 22 21 20 19 18 17

Photos ©: cover snake: Rolf Nussbaumer Photography/Alamy Images; cover background: Givaga/iStockphoto; back cover meerkat: kristianbell/Getty Images; back cover scorpion: Mikhail Egorov/Shutterstock, Inc.; back cover camel: LucVi/Shutterstock, Inc.; back cover background: FRIEDRICHSMEIER/Alamy Images; cloud vector throughout: Freepik.com; 1: Michael Marquand/Getty Images; 2-3: Martin Harvey/Getty Images; 5: Anton Petrus/Shutterstock, Inc.; 7: Steve & Dave Maslowski/Getty Images; 9 background: FRIEDRICHSMEIER/Alamy Images; 9 meerkats: kristianbell/Getty Images; 11 sky: Realimage/Alamy Images; 11 main: Rick & Nora Bowers/Alamy Images; 11 cactus: Dmitry/Fotolia; 13 background: FLPA/Alamy Images; 13 main: Mikhail Egorov/Shutterstock, Inc.; 14-15 left camel: LucVi/Shutterstock, Inc.; 15 right camel: Bernd Bieder/Getty Images; 15 background: Michael Marquand/Getty Images; 17 main: Joel Sartore/Getty Images; 17 sky: Martin Harvey/Getty Images; 19 meerkats: Thomas Dressler/Getty Images; 19 hare: Robert J. Ross/Getty Images; 19 background: Markus Obländer/Getty Images; 19 camel: LucVi/Shutterstock, Inc.; 19 scorpion: Mikhail Egorov/Shutterstock, Inc.; 19 roadrunner: Steve & Dave Maslowski/Getty Images; 19 sidewinder: Rick & Nora Bowers/Alamy Images; 20 left, center right plants: photka/Thinkstock; 20 center left plant: sirichai2514/Depositphotos; 20 right plant: vaeenma/Depositphotos; 20 sidewinder: Rick & Nora Bowers/Alamy Images; 20 roadrunner: Steve & Dave Maslowski/Getty Images; 20 meerkats: Thomas Dressler/Getty Images; 21 center right plant: manub/Depositphotos; 21 left plant: vaeenma/Depositphotos; 21 center left plant: DNY59/Getty Images; 21 right plant: Dmitry/Fotolia; 21 scorpion: Mikhail Egorov/Shutterstock, Inc.; 21 camel: LucVi/Shutterstock, Inc.; 21 hare: Robert J. Ross/Getty Images; 23 center bottom: jacobeukman/Thinkstock; 23 bottom: Anton Petrus/Shutterstock, Inc.; 23 center: Markus Obländer/Getty Images; 23 center top: Michael Marquand/Getty Images; 23 top: Mikhail Egorov/Shutterstock, Inc.

# table of contents

# Welcome to the desert

Every bug, **rodent**, rabbit, and rattler
in our **habitat** soaks up the sun.
If you would like to meet in the shimmering
heat of the desert, come join in the fun!

The world's deserts cover about one-third of Earth's surface.

# roadrunner

I am a bird who enjoys going “cuckoo”
for the lizards and snakes I devour.
But I much prefer sprinting to flying:
I can run twenty miles per hour!

A roadrunner leaves
X-shaped tracks in the sand.
It has two toes facing forward
and two facing back.

# meerkat

My family of twenty or more
is known as a "gang" or a "mob."
We watch out for eagles and jackals
and cobras because that's our job.

At night, meerkats like to snuggle up together. They sleep in a big pile.

# sidewinder rattlesnake

I make lines like zigzaggy S's
on **dunes** along this golden land.
When my belly is full, then I wind up
and disappear deep in the sand.

Sidewinders have a venomous bite. They hunt small animals such as rats and rabbits.

# scorpion

I may seem like a miniature lobster
but my **burrow** is not in the ocean.
What accounts for my fearsome appearance
are my looks and my locomotion!

Adult scorpions live alone in burrows dug in the sand.

# camel

The Dromedary has one hump,
the Bactrian has two.
It is easy to forget this rule,
so here is what to do:
Roll the first initial
over on its flat behind:
The Dromedary is different
from the Bactrian kind.

Camels' humps contain fat. They use it for energy when food is scarce. As the fat gets used up, the humps droop.

# black-tailed jackrabbit

Ask a hawk, owl, fox, or coyote,
"Name your favorite fast-food dessert."
They will say the "American desert hare"—
That is me! I am on constant alert!

The jackrabbit has huge ears. They help control the hare's body temperature.

# hidden homes

In this **vast** playground of wind and sky, you are bound to discover a friend or two, but it may take a while and a very sharp eye to see shy desert animals come into view.

The animals shown in this book are hiding in this desert scene. Can you find them all?

# fact files

| | Roadrunner | Meerkat | Sidewinder Rattlesnake |
|---|---|---|---|
| HOW BIG AM I? | about 22 inches tall *(twice as tall as a robin)* | about 12 inches tall *(the same as a ruler)* | up to 32 inches long *(almost as long as a yardstick)* |
| HOW MUCH DO I WEIGH? | about 10 ounces *(six candy bars)* | about 2 pounds *(two soccer balls)* | 1 pound *(a football)* |
| WHAT DO I EAT? | small mammals, reptiles, insects | insects, fruit, lizards, birds | rodents, lizards, birds |

| Scorpion | Camel<br>Dromedary & Bactrian | Black-Tailed Jackrabbit |
|---|---|---|
| up to 12 inches long *(as long as a ruler)* | up to 6.6 **(D)** or 5.9 **(B)** feet tall at the shoulder *(taller than some grown-ups)* | up to 2 feet tall *(two rulers)* |
| up to 3.5 ounces *(a deck of cards)* | up to 1,500 pounds **(D)** or 1,100 pounds **(B)** *(about three times as much as a gorilla)* | up to 9 pounds *(about the same as a housecat)* |
| insects | grasses, plants | grasses, cacti and other plants |

# deserts...the dry facts

1. **A desert does not have to be hot.** It just has to be dry! There are two types of deserts on Earth: hot and cold. Hot deserts sometimes get small amounts of rain. Cold deserts get small amounts of snow.
2. **The world's largest cold desert is Antarctica.** The coldest temperature ever recorded there was -135.8°Fahrenheit (-94.7°Celsius). Just imagine: Your freezer is 0°Fahrenheit (-18°Celsius). Antarctica is 135 degrees colder!
3. **The world's largest hot desert is the Sahara in northern Africa.** It is about as big as the entire United States.
4. **Hot desert plants are used to living with small amounts of water.** They spread their roots out very wide just under the soil, and have very small leaves. This helps them conserve water.
5. **An oasis is a small area of standing water surrounded by hot desert.** Travelers and animals love to rest and drink water under the shade of its trees and plants!

# glossary

**burrow** (BUR-oh): A tunnel or hole in the ground made or used as a home by a rabbit or other animal.

**dunes** (DOONZ): Small hills formed by the wind or tides.

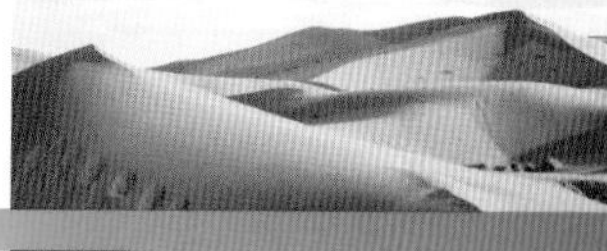

**habitat** (HAB-uh-tat): The place where a plant or animal usually lives or grows.

**rodent** (ROH-duhnt): A small mammal with large, sharp front teeth that constantly grow and are used for gnawing.

**vast** (VAST): Very large in extent or amount.

# index



# facts for now

Visit this Scholastic Web site to learn more about deserts and download the Teaching Guide for this series: **www.factsfornow.scholastic.com**
Enter the keyword **Deserts**

# about the author

**J. Patrick Lewis** has published 100 children's picture and poetry books to date, with a wide variety of publishers. The Poetry Foundation named him the third U.S. Children's Poet Laureate.